Original title:
A Room in My Heart

Copyright © 2025 Creative Arts Management OÜ
All rights reserved.

Author: Levi Montgomery
ISBN HARDBACK: 978-1-80587-170-5
ISBN PAPERBACK: 978-1-80587-640-3

Whispers of an Inner Sanctuary

In the corner, a sock does hide,
A raccoon, my heart's faithful guide.
With laughter brewed in a coffee cup,
We play hide and seek, never give up.

A squeaky chair tells tales of snores,
While pizza boxes pile like mighty shores.
Each giggle echoes, a playful tune,
Bouncing off walls, morning to noon.

Echoes in My Chest

There's a frog, he thinks he's a king,
Croaking out his royal bling.
My heart's a dance floor, never still,
With prancing beats that give a thrill.

A rubber plant wears a silly hat,
It makes me chuckle, imagine that!
With every thump, my spirit glees,
Each silly moment frames the breeze.

The Chamber of Tender Secrets

A teddy bear who tells me jokes,
In whispers soft, he giggles, pokes.
We share our snacks, he steals my fries,
With marshmallow dreams and candy skies.

The closet's filled with secrets spun,
Of plastic swords and fights for fun.
Pillow forts rise, like castles bright,
A kingdom built on pure delight.

Nook of Forgotten Dreams

Beneath the bed, a monster sleeps,
He snores so loud, it makes me weep.
But when he wakes, he's friendly still,
With tales of chaos to fulfill.

The bookshelf holds my squishy toys,
Comics, games, and silly noise.
In every crack, a giggle wakes,
My heart's own laughter, it never breaks.

The Haven of Vulnerable Truths

There's a place where socks go to hide,
Amidst the clutter, by the laundry tide.
Old love notes scribbled with playful sighs,
Echoing whispers, like playful lies.

It's home to my sad plant on the shelf,
When folks ask about it, I joke, "It's a self!"
In this chaos, my heart takes the cake,
A hall of mirrors can't help but shake.

Cushions argue over who takes the throne,
While my cat claims the prime spots alone.
Karaoke nights with the bathroom's fine tunes,
Hideaway of giggles beneath the moons.

If walls could giggle, they'd laugh till they burst,
Sharing my secrets from worst to the first.
This sanctuary wears mismatched shoes,
Dancing with shadows, a place of few blues.

Enclave of Past Embraces

In corners dusty where the echoes hide,
Memories bounce, no reason to bide.
An old teddy bear with a wobbly eye,
Laughs at my awkward, cringy replies.

On shelves, old trophies of games long ago,
Dusty, but proudly they steal the show.
I ask the trophies, 'Are you proud of my streak?'
They nod with a grin, though they're quite antique.

These walls have seen love socks tussling in fray,
A romance within the board games we play.
Our laughter still lingers like the scent of pie,
In my nostalgic nook, where time surely flies.

Each book is a friend who won't tell my lies,
Pages flipping, revealing old ties.
In this enclave, you'll find quirky delight,
Where silly and sweet dance through the night.

The Heart's Mosaic

Here's a patchwork quilt of misfit tales,
Stitched with laughter, where sanity fails.
Socks that don't match and cups with a chip,
In this colorful chaos, I love to trip.

Each corner's a canvas of memories dear,
With a splash of the weirdness that makes me cheer.
Pastel sticky notes with doodles galore,
A visual feast, it's never a bore.

There's a chair that squeaks like it knows my thoughts,
And a window that winks when I share my rot.
Just when I think it's all falling apart,
The jigsaw of life makes a fine work of art.

With laughter as paint, my heart feels alive,
Every quirk tells a story, helps me to thrive.
In this colorful mess, there's room for a laugh,
A whimsical maze, my odd little half.

Serene Hideaway of Emotion

In a nook laden with mismatched dreams,
Socks perform ballet in moonlight beams.
A clock ticks softly, but never on cue,
While my walls listen in on the ruckus that's true.

Brooms play the cello, dust bunnies dance,
In my cozy retreat, things happen by chance.
A cookie jar hoarder with treats just in sight,
Says, "Share if you dare—a sweetened delight!"

Here's where my heart beats to a comical tune,
With laughter as spicy as a cartoon moon.
Pillows conspire in pillow fights bold,
As I twirl in my blanket fortress of gold.

This sanctuary filled with giggles and cheer,
Bears witness to stories, some silly, some dear.
In the calm of the chaos, I take a deep breath,
In this playful hideaway, I find happiness.

Footprints in the Dust

When I walk through my heart's hall,
I find odd socks and a rubber ball.
There are footprints left by old pizza,
And giggles trapped in a silly visa.

In corners lurk my childhood toys,
They whisper secrets, make silly noise.
A vacuum thinks it's on a spree,
But it only rows through my history.

Every drawer, a treasure chest,
Filled with dreams, maybe a jest.
I never know what I'll uncover,
Perhaps a howl or giggle to recover.

Yet in this messy, joyful space,
I find warmth in each silly trace.
So I'll dance in the dust, don't mind the mess,
In the chaos of love, I'm truly blessed.

The Heart's Diary

I opened up my heart's thick book,
Found pages filled with a sly little crook.
He doodled hearts and scribbled dreams,
In ink splotches and silly memes.

Dear diary, today was a blast,
Wrote about that time I tripped and passed.
With laughter spilling from every line,
Turns out love's a real goldmine!

Each entry's a comedy show,
With punchlines that steal the heart's glow.
Tales of silly crushes, wild and grand,
My diary's where joy takes a stand.

But sometimes it gets a bit silly,
Like my dress that turned out frilly.
Through all the chaos, a grin appears,
In this madcap world, love sneers and cheers.

Bridges of Understanding

We built bridges from laughter and jests,
With planks of puns and silly quests.
Each beam's a moment shared in fun,
Connecting hearts, two as one.

Crossing over is quite a treat,
With goofy shoes on my happy feet.
A dance in the middle, a wobbly jig,
Chasing after dreams, we dance a big gig.

On either side, waves of cheer,
Shouting jokes loud enough to hear.
The bridge may shake and bend with glee,
But it holds strong with camaraderie.

So let's stroll across, hand in hand,
Each step's a laugh, perfectly planned.
As long as we share our funny lore,
These bridges thrive forevermore.

Shadows of Longing

In the corners of my heart, shadows play,
They twist and twirl in a wacky ballet.
A longing for snacks and cozy nights,
Filled with laughter and funny flights.

I see shadows of friends long past,
Dancing with cookies, having a blast.
Their giggles echo against the wall,
Spinning tales of our crazy brawl.

Each shadow whispers a silly joke,
As I sip my milk and munch on a poke.
The shadows know all my funny sides,
As the heart's stage where laughter abides.

So let them prance and swirl with cheer,
In this shadow world, we hold so dear.
For in this space of silly dreams,
I find joy bursting at the seams.

The Heart's Gallery

My heart's a gallery of odd balloons,
With goofy clowns and dancing raccoons.
A portrait of love, mismatched and bright,
Each frame has a giggle that tickles the night.

Canvas of smiles, glitter galore,
Swinging on swings with a laughter encore.
Paint drips like joy, a colorful spree,
A masterpiece crafted, just for me!

Chamber of Tenderness

In my cozy nook of silly delight,
There's a sock puppet hosting a tea party tonight.
Cups full of jelly and laughter so sweet,
We toast to the joy that can't be beat.

A warm fuzzy blanket wrapped with a grin,
Hugs from old teddy bears tucked right in.
Each corner's a chuckle, each shadow a tease,
Where giggles bloom gently just like the breeze.

Faded Photographs and Dreamscapes

Old photos of cats wearing hats so grand,
Acrobatic mice performing on demand.
A snapshot of joy, where whimsy reigns,
With postcards from dreams tangled up in chains.

Pictures of gnomes at the beach in the sun,
Splashing in puddles, oh what fun!
Each grainy moment a slip in time,
Where laughter and silliness always rhyme.

Echoing Laughter

Silent whispers dance with each shout,
As the echoes of laughter repeatedly sprout.
A symphony played by the quirkiest crew,
With ducklings in tuxedos, just for a view.

In this hall of chuckles, all silly and bright,
The punchlines take flight, oh what a sight!
Jokes tumble like leaves in an autumn parade,
Where giggles are captured, never to fade.

Secret Garden of Sentiments

Amidst the weeds of laughter's grasp,
I planted seeds of quirky dreams.
The gnomes all dance in top hats bold,
While butterflies sip tea with beams.

In this patch of joy, I find my muse,
With sunshine spilling jokes from trees.
The daisies giggle at my shoes,
While squirrels barter nuts for cheese.

Petunias wear their finest hats,
Telling tales of fanciful quests.
While bees compete in silly spats,
And daisies whisper secret tests.

In this garden where smiles bloom,
My heart's a lively comedy.
With every whim and joyful tune,
Each petal's painted memory.

Grotto of Fleeting Moments

In a cave of chuckles and silly tales,
Echoes bounce from wall to wall.
Here, laughter swings like dangling pails,
And hiccups bubble, rise, and fall.

Stalactites drip with jokes untold,
While shadows dance in playful glee.
My heart, a treasure, sparkles bold,
As echoes claim their territory.

Potted plants wear grins that charm,
As I sip on a giggle brew.
The air is thick with silly balm,
While moments tease and twist anew.

In these halls of whimsy, bright,
Fleeting moments charm the night.

The Den of Heartfelt Echoes

A cozy nook where chuckles cling,
And cushions whisper sweet goodbyes.
With every snicker, heartstrings sing,
Beneath a ceiling of surprise.

Mirthful echoes bounce around,
As pillows giggle, freshly stuffed.
In this den, joy knows no bound,
And tickles chase away the gruff.

Framed memories play hide and seek,
While laughter drips from every crack.
This haven's warmth, a cozy peak,
Where silly tales make mirth unpack.

Here, heartbeats dance in rhythmic throngs,
As joy transforms the mundane wrongs.

Labyrinth of Lost Connections

A maze of giggles, twists, and turns,
Where paths connect with quirky smiles.
Each corner hides a lesson learned,
In playful antics, endless miles.

Wandering through this tangled place,
I stumble on a joke once told.
With laughter sprouting in each space,
Lamenting moments not so cold.

The walls are lined with memories bright,
And every bend brings forth a thrill.
Each mishap painted in pure light,
As heart and humor find their will.

In this labyrinth, joy's the key,
Unlocking every whimsy spree.

Whispers of Solace

In the corner, there's a chair,
It squeaks and creaks, it's full of flair.
A cat is snoring, loud and proud,
While I just sip on tea—how loud!

The pictures wave like friends at war,
They giggle as I trip on the floor.
A dust bunny dances, takes a stand,
And claims the space as its own land.

The clock is ticking, mocking me,
As time slips by so carelessly.
But in this chaos, sweet delight,
I chuckle softly through the night.

So here I stay, this funny scene,
With all my quirks, I reign as queen.
Embracing laughter, so divine,
In this odd haven, joy's my line.

Timeless Reflections

Mirrors laugh, their glassy cheer,
I check my hair—oh no, a deer!
A sage once said, 'Don't take a peek,'
Yet here I am, feeling quite chic.

The clock thumbs through moments' pages,
Counting the years like wine in cages.
I shout at time, 'Just chill a bit!'
And dance with shadows, I won't quit.

Each photo tells a tale untold,
With shirts so bright, they seem quite bold.
Yet here I giggle, hand on heart,
In timeless fun, we'll never part.

So here's to laughter, bright and free,
In this reflection, just you and me.
With every tick, a silly chase,
We'll laugh through time at this odd place.

The Seed of Connection

A potted plant, it winks at me,
With leafy arms so wild and free.
I talk to it like a best friend,
It nods along, on that I depend.

There's mischief here, that's clear as day,
The parrot mimics what I say.
"Let's dance!" I shout, and off we go,
While neighbors stare with eyes aglow.

A sock on the floor, a shoe askew,
Connections bloom in chaos—who knew?
From tiny seeds, big laughs arise,
In tangled roots, friendship lies.

So plant your joys, your quirks, your glee,
Inside these walls, it's wild and free.
With every laugh, we're growing fast,
Bound by the silliness that will last.

Lullabies of the Heart

Socks on the ceiling? What a sight!
The laundry laughs, oh, what a plight!
My bedtime stories are full of snore,
Yet here I am, wanting more.

A lullaby that breaks all rules,
With dancing spoons and singing mules.
The sheep outside wear polka dots,
A bedtime tale that hits the spots.

At midnight's hour, my giggles swell,
As jars of cookies start to yell.
In dreams, they dance, so sweet and light,
While I laugh loud through the night.

So tuck me in with glee and cheer,
As silly whispers fill my ear.
In this odd serenade I dwell,
Sweet lullabies cast a humorous spell.

A Haven for Dreams

In the corner sits my chair,
With crumpled snacks and fluffy hair.
A kingdom ruled by stray cat's reign,
With laughter echoing, never plain.

The lights flicker like a disco ball,
My socks have staged a 'sock-it-all.'
And on the wall, a portrait of cheese,
Because even dreams deserve some freeze.

Each pillow's piled higher than the sky,
Where the unicorns and penguins fly.
In this space of whimsy and delight,
I swear reality takes a flight.

So come on in, leave your shoes at the door,
Where goofy giggles and snacks galore.
In this sanctuary of my own design,
Each moment sparkles, and truly, I shine.

Windows to the Soul

Peeking through my life's big panes,
I see the cat plotting all my gains.
It swats at dust, oh what a feat,
Like a fuzzy ninja on tiny feet.

The neighbors argue 'bout the fence,
I watch their drama, so intense.
With popcorn ready, I take a seat,
Their loud debates? A comic treat.

I wipe the glass to make it clear,
What's happening out there, oh dear!
A dog has stolen someone's shoe,
And now it's running, who knew?

Through these panes, my mind does wander,
Each glance outside—my heart grows fonder.
In silliness, life's colors bloom,
Through the eyes of my windowed room.

The Canvas of Connection

On canvas bright with splashes wide,
Are doodles of my silly pride.
A stick figure's arm does flip and flop,
While brushes twirl, and colors pop.

The paint's a mix of laughter's hue,
And under it, a secret clue.
For in each stroke, I find a friend,
With quirky limbs that twist and bend.

A masterpiece of joyful cheer,
Each drop of paint, a hearty cheer.
With mustaches drawn on every face,
Even the dogs have joined this race!

So hang it high, let it gleam,
This canvas tells a silly dream.
With colors bright and friendship near,
In every laugh, I feel sincere.

Reverberations of Love

In tiny echoes, whispers play,
Where my socks dance at the end of the day.
They waltz around, a funny sight,
Who knew laundry could bring such light?

The fridge hums sweet melodies bold,
While leftovers plot to never grow old.
Each bite a serenade, a funny food band,
In this feast of laughter, all is grand.

The walls are covered with sticky notes,
Reminders of laughter, inside jokes that float.
'Don't forget the cake—make friends with the pie!'
In this joyous space, we reach for the sky.

Here love's a tune, quirky and bright,
It dances and twirls, a pure delight.
In echoes that bounce, I find my way,
In the symphony of each silly day.

The Heart's Infinite Canvas

There's a space for cake and fun,
With frosting dreams, oh what a run!
A dance floor made of laughter bright,
Where silly hats can take to flight.

Cushions soft, a comfy chair,
For napping cats without a care.
The walls adorned with jokes on strings,
A gallery of silly things.

In the corner, a tiny fridge,
Stocked with snacks, the ultimate bridge.
Every bite is a burst of cheer,
Brought together over a beer.

So when you step inside my chest,
Expect some giggles, just the best.
A heart that beats with joy and glee,
You'll find a world of whimsy free.

Within My Embrace

Nestled snug like a biscuit warm,
This cozy spot is quite the charm.
A quilt of smiles, mismatched socks,
Silly faces tick on the clocks.

Where tickles happen without warning,
And every day starts with a morning.
Hot chocolate mugs in hand we share,
Giant marshmallows float in air.

A place of games and joy loud and clear,
Dance-offs spark up, bring on the cheer.
With silly routines that we rehearse,
There's always room for one more verse.

So if you're ever feeling low,
Step right in, let the fun flow.
Within these walls, a soft embrace,
Laughter lives; it's a happy space.

Echoes of Affection

Hear the chuckles bounce off the walls,
As goofy antics create loud calls.
A karaoke mic for the brave and bold,
Singing tunes that never grow old.

Socks that dance and slippers that glide,
In this delight, we all can slide.
The echoes ring of ticklish fights,
Under colorful, twinkly lights.

Photos hang with funny faces,
Captured laughs in cozy places.
Every glance tells a tale so sweet,
With goofy poses and happy feet.

So when the world gets far too dense,
Join me here for a dose of tense.
We'll echo fondness, laugh and play,
In this haven where joy holds sway.

Whispered Memories

Whispers float like popcorns popping,
In corners where the jokes are hopping.
Capacity for giggles galore,
With stories shared, we can't ignore.

The rug that dances under our feet,
Each step is silly, can't be beat.
We'll chase the shadows 'til it's night,
With merry minds, we take to flight.

A scrapbook full of quirks and tales,
Nonsense moments, like jumping whales.
With every turn of the yellowed page,
We find pure joy at every age.

So remember this when the day is grim,
Slip inside, let the light not dim.
In whispered moments we create,
A treasure chest that's never late.

Hidden Corners of Solitude

In the dusty nook where socks reside,
A gentle ghost of laughter hides.
It tickles my toes when I sit alone,
As I ponder the snacks I won't bemoan.

A chair with a spine that creaks and whines,
Holds secrets of snacks and outdated pines.
The cat gives a glance, like, 'What's your deal?'
While I invent stories for every meal.

The window whispers tales of the weird,
As moths join the dance, quite unappeared.
I giggle at them, they fly with a flair,
In this wild party of solitude, I swear.

A plant by the wall, looking slightly blue,
Wonders why I haven't watered it too.
But honestly, it's just a touch too bright,
And my hidden corner feels just right!

Sanctuary of Sentiments

Within these walls where my thoughts collide,
A couch holds the weight of my dreams inside.
It swallows my snacks, my burdens it shares,
While reminding me of all my crazy lairs.

The curtains flutter like they're on a date,
With sunlight that teases, never too late.
It's the perfect spot for my wildest schemes,
While coffee spills over my best-laid dreams.

A calendar filled with awkward grins,
Marks days of mischief, my little wins.
Like when I spilled soup while trying to pose,
For selfies that bruised my fabric of clothes.

So here I revel, just me and my thoughts,
In a space that collects all my vibrant knots.
While the world outside spins, a noisy ballet,
I chuckle at life from my cozy café!

Nurtured by Nostalgia

Old toys stacked high like towers of gold,
Unraveled stories from when I was bold.
Each action figure waving a hand,
Screams 'Take us back!' to that distant land.

Posters of bands that I've never seen,
Mock my taste in music, I'll be honest, mean.
Yet cranking the tunes makes me dance around,
In this mad disco of memories found.

A mirror reflects all the cringe-worthy years,
Where hairstyles were bold and laughter sincere.
Each wrinkle a badge, each spot a smile,
In my nostalgic nook, I could stay awhile.

I sit and I ponder what's next in the queue,
With a tub of ice cream and a Netflix review.
This trove of delight wraps me in glee,
A place for the past and a future to see!

Sheltered Affections

A pile of clothes that resemble a mound,
In my fortress of fluff, I'm jovially crowned.
Draped like a blanket, they keep me so warm,
As I plot how to build my next chaotic charm.

A dog-eared book rests on the floor,
With tales of adventure, it begs to explore.
Coffee stains tell stories of nights filled with cheer,
While I giggle at memories, oh so dear.

The fridge hums a tune that seriously sways,
With leftovers dancing through hazy displays.
A yogurt that's healing from last week's delight,
Mocks my ambitions with each passing bite.

So here I confine my quirkiest dreams,
In a den of affection, it's not what it seems.
With each playful moment, I build and I grow,
In this sheltered haven, I steal the show!

Quiet Spaces of Belonging

In a corner, a cat does snooze,
Beneath my pile of mismatched shoes.
Finding treasures like a wayward sock,
Who knew my closet would host such a flock?

Pet goldfish don't talk much at all,
Except for when they tape it to the wall.
My plants argue on who's the best,
While I giggle at their leafy jest.

A spoon's lost, in the depths of the drawer,
It might just be plotting to explore.
The fridge hums a tune, soft and low,
Guess it's rehearsing for the show!

So welcome, dear friends, to this silly space,
Where laughter and chaos set the pace.
Though secrets and oddments fill the air,
This is the place where I'll always share!

Thorns and Blossoms

In the garden where roses can bite,
I giggle and dance, avoiding the fright.
The daisies gossip about the weeds,
While bees can't commit to their buzzing deeds.

Thorns point out what's tough in love,
While blossoms are the quips from above.
A snail slowly wins on this leafy ride,
We laugh as he takes a wrong turn and slides.

I planted some seeds, hoping for cheer,
But all that sprouted was an old shoe here.
This chaos of nature brings me delight,
With blooms that just seem like pure oversight!

So cheers to the garden we all can share,
With thorns that poke and buds that glare.
A riot of colors, a comical sight,
In a world with laughs, everything feels right!

The Hearth of Yearning

A fire crackles in the heart of the room,
While marshmallows dance, spellbinding their doom.
The chairs are all wobbly, in a fine old state,
I laugh as they creak, tell tales of fate.

Toasts drift and wander 'round the warm glow,
Each one more burnt than the last, I know.
Socks on the mantle, they've lost their pairs,
Who knew fashion would lead to such glares?

The evening's filled with silly old tales,
About mishaps with bikes and forgotten pails.
With laughter and flavor, our hearts intertwine,
Our love's a bright spark that makes us all shine.

So here's to the warmth on a chilly night,
Sharing our stories, oh what a delight!
With a side of cringes and marshmallow fluff,
In this cozy nook, we can't get enough!

Threads of Intimacy

In a quilt stitched with laughter and dreams,
We find our rhythm, or so it seems.
The threads are tangled in a curious dance,
While jokes fly around, not left to chance.

Each patch tells a tale of old blunders,
Of socks in the dryer that vanish like thunder.
In whispers we share our evenings' delight,
While popcorn jumps up for a comedic flight.

Silly secrets lie under each fold,
A treasure of giggles worth more than gold.
As we weave the fabric with joy and jest,
This tapestry blooms, making us feel blessed.

So let's raise a glass to these crazy ties,
To the fun little moments that never die.
In this woven warmth, our hearts skip and race,
Each thread binds us closer in this funny place!

Atrium of Unspoken Love

In a corner lurks a sock,
It dances like a silly clock.
With crumbs and dust, it plays the fool,
A jester's hat, my love's own rule.

The chair sings songs of old romance,
As cat and dog engage in dance.
A vase of flowers proudly snickers,
Its petals laugh at all my snickers.

The fridge hums tunes of joy and cheer,
While leftovers whirl, it rules the sphere.
A sandwich dated '93 remains,
Laughs with me through all loves' pains.

In this fun nook, we crack a smile,
Where love is awkward, yet worthwhile.
With jokes and giggles all around,
In this space, true joy is found.

Shadows of the Soul

In shadows lurking, dreams take flight,
A goblin steals my pizza slice.
My heart, a workshop of my fears,
Tickles me with laughter and tears.

A broom insists it's got a voice,
It sweeps away my inner noise.
The curtains gossip without care,
They share my secrets, unaware.

With every creak, my floorboards tease,
They squeak like mice searching for cheese.
The nighttime moon winks at my plight,
And whispers jokes to make it bright.

In this dim dance of love and jest,
I find my heart, it feels the best.
Where shadows play and spirits twirl,
Each giggle is a love-filled pearl.

A Cove of Gentle Whispers

In corners, whispers do reside,
Like fish that swim and start to slide.
They tickle with a secret joke,
As laughter bursts from every poke.

The lamp flickers with a grin so sly,
It flicks and flirts, oh me, oh my!
The cushions giggle, soft as clouds,
Their muffled chuckles, loud and proud.

Within these walls, the echoes play,
Like children on a rainy day.
A teapot's whistle joins the cheer,
As we sip stories, crystal clear.

This cozy nook, a laughing space,
With warmth and jokes, and love's embrace.
A cove of whispers, soft and neat,
Where joy and humor joyfully meet.

Vault of Hidden Hopes

In this vault, my dreams are stacked,
With broken toys and laughter packed.
Each hope wears socks, mismatched, of course,
As wishes spill out with gentle force.

The mirror jokes, reflects my face,
It twists and turns, a playful race.
My clothes conspire, they plot and schee,
To wear the colors no one can see.

Behind a door, my garden grows,
With daisies trying on their clothes.
The sunbeams dance, they giggle bright,
As shadows play in morning light.

In this vault, I've saved some cheer,
For love and laughter always near.
With every hope, a giggle springs,
In this treasure, joy forever clings.

Attic of Tender Recollections

In the attic, I found my old sock,
A relic of days when I'd break every clock.
Dust bunnies dance like they're in a parade,
Chasing memories of mischief I made.

I stumbled on letters from my pet cat,
Who claimed my snacks and took a long nap.
Piles of old toys, all covered in grime,
They whisper, "Remember our glorious crime?"

There's a mirror where I once struck a pose,
Thought I was cool, why no one knows.
Reflections of laughter echo all around,
In this silly place, pure joy is found.

So here I'll stay, amidst clutter and charms,
With each goofy memory, I rest in their arms.
Life's ups and downs, I'll take with a cheer,
In this attic, I'm king; I've nothing to fear.

The Heartbeat's Whisper

Tick-tock goes my quirky heart's beat,
It dances along to the tune of my feet.
A whisper so soft, like a joke in the night,
Tickling my senses with pure delight.

The rhythm of laughter, it echoes so clear,
As I juggle my worries and sip on good cheer.
Funny how worries can bounce off the wall,
A pogo stick heart that refuses to stall.

With each silly thought, I'm light on my toes,
Like a wiggly worm in a garden that grows.
My heartbeat's a drummer, in a band of delight,
Playing all day, and grooving all night.

So I'll chuckle and grin, let the world slip by,
With a heartbeat that giggles, oh me, oh my!
In the quiet of whispers, I feel so alive,
In this silly symphony, I thrive and I jive.

Alcove of Unforgotten Joys

In a nook where the sunlight loves to play,
Wonders and giggles invite me to stay.
Old photo albums with wild outfits in sight,
Remind me of dances that dared the moonlight.

Sticky notes scribbled with plans for a feast,
Halos of joy, I'd wear like a beast.
Inside this alcove, silliness reigns,
Replaying the moments that tickle my brains.

Here's a plush bear, wearing my socks,
He whispers sweet secrets while guarding the clocks.
A treasure chest filled with dreams from the past,
In this spot full of laughter, my heart beats the fastest.

I'll sip on the sunshine and giggle aloud,
In this alcove of joys, I'll always feel proud.
With friends made of laughter that never grow old,
These unforgotten joys are worth their weight in gold.

Chamber of Solitary Reflection

In my chamber, a throne made of dreams,
With curtains of laughter and sunlight beams.
Reflecting on moments that tickle my spout,
Even my shadow has a funny way out.

Doodles of dragons swirl 'round my head,
Each one a joke that my pet goldfish said.
The echoes of giggles are ringing so clear,
Even the silence joins in with a cheer!

Here lies a pillow that's grown quite a mind,
Whispering stories of the wild and unkind.
I'll laugh with my echoes, they're my best mates,
In this chamber of ponderings, joy never abates.

So here I retreat from the rush of the world,\nIn my castle
of quirky, new thoughts are unfurled.
With humor as armor and wit as my guide,
In this chamber, I flourish, I shine with great pride.

Oasis of Calm

In the corner, a cactus sits,
Wearing a hat that usually fits.
A goldfish is plotting its big escape,
While I'm dreaming of cake on a lovely drape.

The pillow fights with my head each night,
Telling me jokes till my dreams take flight.
A blanket fort made of mismatched sheets,
Hosts the finest of imaginary treats.

A spider spins tales in a ball of thread,
While the clock insists I should be in bed.
My slippers are still trying to find their mate,
But they say, "Let's dance, it's never too late!"

Lampshades giggle with light-hearted cheer,
As I whisper secrets that no one can hear.
This silly little space, oh what a fun part,
It's the jolliest place inside my own heart.

Keepsakes of Love

A jar of buttons, a rusted key,
A picture of me at age three.
My teddy wears sunglasses, what a sight!
He's probably dreaming of a disco night.

Postcards from friends who never arrive,
Each with a tale that makes me revive.
Old letters flutter like butterflies free,
They whisper sweet nothings, just to tease me.

A rubber duck from a long-lost game,
Keeps all my secrets, does it feel shame?
The old lamp has stories in every glare,
Of late-night snacks and a messy hair affair.

With each quirky trinket, my heart does swell,
In this wonderland, all's well, all's well.
It's a circus of laughter that fills the space,
Every keepsake a joke in this lovable place.

A Gaze Through the Veil

Behind the curtain, a cat takes a peek,
Wishing for mice, a feast of the week.
The plants are all gossiping, what a sight,
As I try to decipher their tiny delight.

A mirror reflects an old sock puppet show,
With dramatic flair, they steal the glow.
The sun sneaks in, playing hide and seek,
Giving my messy hair a little tweak.

A basket of laundry—good grief, what's this?
It's a monster, I swear, or perhaps just bliss?
With each little glance, my heart starts to dance,
It's a whimsical world, full of pure chance.

Laughter echoes in every small crack,
In this bubbly abode where I never look back.
Every gaze through the veil makes me grin wide,
For in this delightful space, I can hide.

The Closet of Dreams

In the closet, a wizard wig thrives,
With capes from the times I played with my lives.
Odd shoes are waiting for their shoes to shine,
While socks without partners sip on sunshine.

A treasure map leading to nowhere at all,
Leads me to chocolate, let's have a ball!
An old broomstick rests, tired from the flight,
Whispering tales of adventures at night.

Coats from the past, they whisper their truth,
Reminiscing the wild pranks of my youth.
A chorus of moths starts to sing their chant,
Should I call them out? Oh, that would be scant!

With twinkles and giggles, this closet is mine,
A land of the silly, where dreams intertwine.
Every time I dive in, I find treasures anew,
In the closet of dreams, laughter shines through.

Heartstrings Unveiled

In the corner sits my sock,
A lonely fate, it still can rock.
A makeshift throne for old karaoke,
Where I sing tunes that aren't so pokey.

A fridge that hums a happy tune,
Reminds me of pizza by noon.
With every bite, laughter takes flight,
Who knew cheese could feel so right?

Old chairs that creak like ancient tales,
Host whispers of my childhood fails.
A dance with ghosts, a giggling spree,
Here you find my comedy spree.

Balloons from last year's birthday bash,
Float like dreams, in wild, bright flash.
Each twist and turn, a memory's tease,
In this wild space, I aim to please.

Refuge of Silent Longing

Beneath the bed, my dust bunnies crawl,
They hold secrets and laughter, that's all.
Their silent giggles, soft like a breeze,
They whisper to me, 'Life's meant to tease.'

The wallflowers bloom in a colorful race,
Each paint splatter holds a funny face.
I trip on laughter, a comic's parade,
In this cozy nook, we all have it made.

A closet that guffaws at my old clothes,
Screaming 'fashion mishaps!' in wrinkled throes.
With each passing trend, it silently sighs,
Yet still holds my joy through all the goodbyes.

In this retreat, I find a soft chair,
That's lived through my dreams and a few wild stares.
It creaks like a friend, who knows too much,
Together we laugh, 'cause life's out of touch.

The Space Where Memories Dwell

A table strewn with crayons and cheer,
Colors of fun, painted younger years.
Each mark a giggle, a joy to recall,
Who knew a scribble could encapsulate all?

The photos hang, in silly array,
Capturing moments, that went astray.
A pie-faced uncle with frosting so bright,
Reminds me that chaos feels just right.

Books piled high, with stories to weave,
A comic relief that makes us believe.
When boredom strikes, the laughter flows,
In this space, imagination grows.

Stickers on walls, a testament proud,
Of whims and giggles, we laughed aloud.
Here lives the magic, in chortles and zest,
In this quirky haven, I feel truly blessed.

Within These Tender Walls

My pillow knows all my secret schemes,
Dreams of grandeur or silly extremes.
Each plump embrace, a bubble of goof,
It keeps me grounded while I chase my hoof.

The lamp flickers in a way that's sly,
It jokes that it's too bright to say goodbye.
I nod along, pretending it's sane,
But it's winking, knowing we both share the fame.

The rug tells tales of clumsy falls,
And how I danced like a goose through stalls.
With a little twist and a spin so grand,
I'd trip and tumble, but no one would stand.

So here I lounge in this joyful cocoon,
Awaiting the laughter as bright as the moon.
Within these tender confines, I feel the spark,
A sanctuary alive, with silly remarks.

The Loft of Emotions

Up on a shelf, my socks do play,
In a dance-off of colors, bright and gay.
Underneath a hat, my secrets sleep,
While my old teddy bear starts to creep.

Dust bunnies dream, hidden away,
Plotting adventures for each new day.
Behind the curtains, the laughter hides,
As the gum drops smile, in their sweet pride.

A rubber duck sings in a chorus of cheer,
While sticky notes gather, year after year.
Spiders are spinning webs of fate,
The more they spin, the more I relate.

In this attic of chuckles, joy takes flight,
With each silly memory, all feels right.
So swing open the door, let the fun unfold,
For this loft of emotions is pure as gold.

Coves of Comfort

In a corner nook, I found my snack,
Chips in a bag, with laughter, no lack.
Chocolate bars swim in a cozy sea,
Telling me tales of sweet jubilee.

Under the blanket, a book starts to snore,
While a cat in slippers plots to explore.
Cushions are giggling, stacked up so high,
As pillows conspire to make clouds fly.

Tea spills tales of adventures past,
While the kettle whistles, loud and fast.
Each sip's a journey, a comedy show,
In this cove, where the good vibes flow.

So grab a chair and let's take a seat,
With all of our favorites, oh what a treat!
In this cubby of comfort, laughter's the theme,
A perfect spot to live the dream.

Chains of Sentiment

Locked away thoughts, in a box so tight,
Bracelets of memories shine so bright.
Each trinket giggles with its own story,
Tales of mishaps mixed with some glory.

A key shaped like a shoe taps on the floor,
Hoping to dance, or maybe encore.
The clock on the wall does a tick-tock dance,
Inviting the jam session, if given a chance.

Old postcards whisper, 'Remember that day?'
As sticky notes shout, 'You're silly, hooray!'
In this chain of thoughts, all feelings blend,
A circus of chuckles with no end.

So let's unlock and set the past free,
In the chains of sentiment, come laugh with me!
For every memory, silly or wise,
Has a sparkle of joy, right before our eyes.

The Wind's Verse

Listen close to the breezy tune,
Whispers of laughter in the afternoon.
A kite caught the wind, took off with glee,
Twirling and swirling, wild and free.

The trees chuckle with leaves that sway,
While dandelions dance, come what may.
A cloud in the sky hides a giggly face,
As it tickles the sun in a playful race.

The breeze drops by with a soft, warm hug,
Telling the flowers, 'You're all just a snug.'
Rabbits hop in a comic parade,
While wind chimes rattle, delightfully swayed.

So heed the call of this whimsical ghost,
A merry reminder of what matters most.
In the wind's verse, our giggles reside,
A symphony of joy, forever our guide.

Murmurs of the Past

Whispers of old socks dive from the shelf,
They giggle at my dance with the broomstick elf.
Memories of snacks, crumbs under the bed,
In my mind's funny circus, where laughter is fed.

A ghost of a cat plays peek-a-boo near,
With a wink and a purr, it has no fear.
Tickles of laughter float through the air,
Echoes of chaos, joy everywhere!

Ketchup stains on the wall tell tales so grand,
Of pizza nights and make-believe bands.
Each memory dangles like a colorful kite,
Floating and flapping, a comical sight.

In the corners of past, mischief resides,
With jellybean rainbows and pickle slide rides.
A symphony of chuckles rings out from the space,
As I trip on nostalgia, a humorous chase.

A Nest of Emotions

In a cozy corner, my feelings do play,
Like squirrels with acorns on a bright sunny day.
Joy wears a hat and tumbles about,
While sadness just hides, trying not to shout.

Anger throws pies, aiming at my shoes,
While laughter does hops and shares a few snooze.
Confusion plays darts with an oversized grin,
Peeking from shadows, it's hard to pin down where to begin!

A feather of joy floats high in the sky,
While grumpiness sulks, and gives a loud sigh.
Happy squirrels dance on a tightrope of cheer,
While worries juggle marshmallows, just not here!

Inside this jumbled nest of delight,
Every emotion plays through day and night.
With a wink and a smile, they stay in their slots,
Creating hilarity, loving their spots.

Candles in the Twilight

Candles flicker softly, casting shadows bold,
As chocolate spills secrets and laughter is told.
The moths do a tango, flirting with light,
While I sit and giggle, avoiding the fright.

Wax drips like honey, with a wink in its flow,
While my cat wears a wig, putting on a show.
The aroma of popcorn mixes with dreams,
In this twilight moment, nothing's as it seems.

Silly jokes whisper through the fading glow,
While dancing shadows put on quite the show.
Crickets are crooning their favorite tune,
As candles giggle under the silvery moon.

In this soft twilight, my heart's a delight,
Filled with warmth and whimsy, everything feels right.
Each flame is a story, a giggly embrace,
Igniting the smiles on this whimsical chase.

Tapestries of Togetherness

In threads of laughter, we weave our delight,
A tapestry blossoming, colors so bright.
Knitted with goofiness, stitches of cheer,
Each line a memory that's vivid and clear.

Crazy patterns swirl, as we fumble and trip,
Threading mismatched socks gives our heartstrings a grip.

A patch here for joy, a knot for the fun,
Each loop holds a story, weaved under the sun.

Moments are tangled, like spaghetti at a feast,
Each twist tells a tale, humor never ceased.
With threads of togetherness, laughter sets sail,
Creating a quilt where jokes never fail.

In this mad creation, with giggles aglow,
We sew our mishaps and blow them to show.
Wrapping our hearts in this colorful art,
Our funny little tapestry, a true work of heart.

A Tidal Pool of Feelings

In a wet and wobbly place,
Jellyfish dance with grace,
Crabs scuttle, wearing their hats,
While seaweed wiggles with winks and spats.

Starfish giggle on their rocky throne,
Splashing water, never alone,
Anemones wave, oh what a sight,
In this pool, everything feels just right.

Seashells whisper their sandy schemes,
Crafting wild, oceanic dreams,
Barnacles argue, quite the show,
In this pool, we let our feelings flow.

So take a dip, come and play,
In this wobbly world, we'll sway,
With each wave, let's lift our glee,
In this tidal flap of jubilee.

Wings of Resilience

A quirky bird with mismatched shoes,
Flaps its wings in canvas blues,
Juggling muffins, oh what a sight,
While dodging a pie in mid-flight!

Squirrels cheer with acorn chants,
As the bird in mid-air prance,
Bouncing back from every fall,
With a giggle, it conquers all!

Chasing dreams and bits of cheese,
Sailing on a warm summer breeze,
It soars high, then dives for fun,
Leaving laughter in the sun.

With a wink and a flappy tease,
This feathered friend does as it please,
Laughing at doubts, shooing away,
With wings that dance in bright ballet.

Hidden Treasures of Care

In a shoebox filled with notes,
And socks that smell like fuzzy goats,
Lies a treasure of silly might,
Care wrapped in laughter, shining bright.

Sticky notes with goofy pies,
A map to find the best mud fries,
Dimples of giggles, warmth so near,
In this messy chest, so full of cheer.

Bubbles float with hearts and stars,
Tickle monsters from Mars,
A jar of hugs, pastel and spry,
Here's our solace, oh my, oh my!

Come dig deep, find what's rare,
Quirks of kindness, everywhere,
Past the socks, and wild hairdos,
Are treasures only friendship views.

The Garden of Solitude

In a garden where giggles grow,
With flowers that tickle and glow,
Butterflies wear hats with flair,
While daisies spin in the air!

Bees hum silly tunes of cheer,
Spreading joy to those who hear,
With petals painted, oh so bright,
They dance in daydreams, pure delight!

A fence of laughter, tall and wide,
Where whispers of secrets confide,
In every corner, bloom and sway,
Funny thoughts frolic and play.

So come, my friend, let's plant some glee,
In this garden, wild and free,
With every chuckle, a new seed sown,
In this patch of joy, we've grown!

Under the Stars of Togetherness

Beneath the sky, we set our sights,
Catching dreams on silly nights.
With laughter loud and snacks to share,
We dance like no one's watching there.

The moon is rolling, full of glee,
While we make up a new decree:
To wear our socks upon our heads,
And giggle softly till we're in beds.

A picnic blanket is our stage,
Where squirrels act like they're the rage.
We swap our tales of clumsy falls,
As fireflies light up friendship's walls.

In this chaos, joy resides,
With a sprinkle of truth and a few wild rides.
So here's to us, the nighttime crew,
Under stars that twinkle, oh so true!

Lanterns of Remembrance

In the attic, dusty tales unfold,
With lanterns bright, and stories bold.
We misplace the cheese and talk of the past,
While giggles echo, unsurpassed.

Old photos slip, like time on a ride,
When Grandma danced with a goofy stride.
We laugh till our bellies twist and ache,
With memories shared, we never break.

A note is found, with doodles quite strange,
From childhood years, when life felt achange.
We hang it high, like trophies worn,
To celebrate bonds that were never torn.

So here we glow, like lantern light,
In corners that shimmer with future bright.
Through each jibe, each playful tease,
We weave together, memories with ease.

Into the Echoes

Inside these walls where laughter meets,
We echo jokes and shuffle our feet.
With each funny blunder, we loudly cheer,
For every mishap brings us near.

Echoes ripple like a river's song,
As we recall where we went wrong.
With pie fights that leave us in a mess,
We embrace our failures, no need to stress.

The whispers of fun hang in the air,
Like a cat stuck in my favorite chair.
We tickle our fancies, with puns that fly,
In this chamber of joy, we can't deny.

So let's embrace each silly line,
In these echoes, our hearts align.
With giggles and cheer, no need to fuss,
We're living a joke—come laugh with us!

A Patchwork of Souls

In this quilt of quirks, we toast with flair,
With mismatched socks, and flowered hair.
A tapestry woven from laughter and tears,
In threads of joy, we dispel all fears.

Our stories stitched with a sprinkle of spice,
With moments that tangle, yet feel so nice.
We quilt our lives with silly regret,
Each patch a reminder—our best is not met.

The comical chaos swirls all around,
In our patchwork hearts, silly truths are found.
We patch the seams with the fabric of fun,
Together we race till the day is done.

Each layer a memory, sewn tight with rhyme,
Our hearts beat together, transcending time.
So here we gather, a motley crew,
In this fabric of friendship, forever true.

Heartfelt Interludes

There's a sock on the floor, not just one,
It's hiding from me, oh what fun!
It calls out for snacks, a true little rogue,
Making laundry days feel like a joke.

My cat thinks my chair is his throne,
He judges my snacks with a heavy groan.
Each bite I take, he narrows his eyes,
As if plotting my fall, oh what a surprise!

Plants in the corner secretly sway,
Dancing to tunes that I did not play.
They gossip and whisper, when I'm not near,
About my sock's fate, or my last sad cheer.

While I sip my coffee, half asleep,
The postman arrives, with promises to keep.
He hands me a letter, a curious sight,
From my grandma, with tales that are out of sight!

The Vessel of Trust

In the cupboard, a jar of odd things,
Paperclips, rubber bands, and old strings.
Each piece a secret, I dare not discern,
But they keep me laughing in every turn.

A spoon that once served something so sweet,
Now my dog thinks it's his best treat.
He carries it proudly, a trophy of yore,
As I wonder what else lies hidden for sure.

The fridge hums a tune, beeping in style,
It's filled with leftovers, all in a pile.
They're concocting a plan to escape their fate,
In a dance-off, they hope to clear the plate.

And on the shelf, a calendar's smile,
Marks every birthday, and each funny trial.
With sticky notes stuck in a colorful mess,
It maps out our love, in a playful jest.

Harmony's Refuge

In my closet hang shoes that don't fit,
Yet I keep them around, isn't that a hit?
They remind me of dance moves, where I'd trip and fall,
A comedic ballet, not graceful at all.

Under the bed, lies a dust bunny clan,
Planning their meetings with an old soda can.
They giggle at me as I clean in a haste,
Protesting their right to a comfortable space.

The mirror reflects, a face full of glee,
I practice my jokes, just the cat and me.
He laughs with his eyes, rolling them in delight,
As I perform for an audience, quiet at night.

With cushions piled high, like a fortress of dreams,
We whisper our secrets through giggles and memes.
In this cozy chaos, joy takes its part,
Where every echo is a beat from the heart.

The Map of Our Affection

On the wall hangs a map, detailed and neat,
Marked with our mishaps, my clumsy defeat.
Every 'X' tells a tale that we share,
Of failed attempts and our spontaneous flair.

Our fridge is a canvas for doodles and notes,
Each drawing a story of wild, silly quotes.
With magnets and laughter, we plot and we plan,
Every meal's an adventure, it's just who we am!

There's a chair with a cushion that's seen better days,
We sit there together, lost in our ways.
With chips on our laps and soda in hand,
Plotting our escape to a fictional land.

In this quirky habitat, love dances around,
In the spills and the giggles, our joy can be found.
It's a treasure map drawn with laughter and cheer,
An atlas of all that we hold oh so dear.

The Shaded Nook

In a cozy corner, with snacks galore,
I hide from chores, like a lion's roar.
The cushions giggle, they crinkle and squeak,
This padded paradise, it's my hide-and-seek.

Mismatched socks dance, in their joyful spree,
Here, a sock puppet claims the right to decree.
The curtains whisper secrets, they know my name,
In this wacky haven, I'm always the same.

A teacup monkey sips his herbal brew,
While rubber ducks waddle, quite a silly crew.
I chuckle and snort, as I sip on my tea,
In my shaded nook, I'm forever carefree.

With laughter as music, I twirl and glide,
In this silly realm, my worries subside.
The clock ticks away, but I'm just too spry,
In this nutshell of joy, I'll laugh 'til I cry.

Essence of Together

Two spoons in a drawer, always side by side,
They giggle and snicker, no need to hide.
They stare at the forks, quite sharp and unkind,
'We're sweeter than sugar, but they're just behind.'

A jellybean jar filled with colors so bright,
They claim to be best friends, oh what a sight!
They bounce in the pantry, tossing beans to each,
While the cereal grumbles, 'Can't you let us teach?'

The blender sings loudly, it's quite a loud cheer,
As the toasters shout, 'Let's toast it right here!'
But it's laughter and kinship that guide our escape,
Essence of together, oh what a great shape!

We nibble on moments, both crunchy and sweet,
With rhythms of giggles, we dance on our feet.
Life's a delightful potluck; bring your own dish,
In this banquet of heart, there's always a wish!

Dreamcatcher of Quietude

Caught in the web of a sleepy old chair,
Dreams spill like popcorn, without a care.
The dust bunnies gather, hold a parade,
As I snooze on the sofa, in my dream escapade.

Whispers of silence, a blanket so warm,
As kittens convene, instructing the charm.
They pounce on the cushions, in pursuit of a nap,
While I join the fold in my magical trap.

Clouds float on by, wearing marshmallow hats,
While I float in slumber with my furry pals' chats.
They cuddle and tumble, they twirl and they spin,
In this dreamcatcher realm, every moment's a win.

Then suddenly—whoosh! I'm back with a start,
The real world's a circus, but I play my part.
I giggle and grin, for dreams are the loot,
In my cozy cocoon of soft slippers and fruit.

Seeds of Heartfelt Moments

In the garden of laughter, we plant our dreams,
Sprouting silly stories, bursting at the seams.
We water them daily with jokes and with mirth,
These seeds of delight bring love to the earth.

Each sunflower giggles at the sun up high,
While daisies wear glasses, just to look sly.
We dance through the petals, our spirits in bloom,
Creating a canvas that brightens the room.

With butterflies prancing, we chuckle and play,
Sharing whimsical tales, come what may.
From quirky cacti with hats made of lace,
To merry little weeds that own this big space.

We harvest the joy, in baskets of cheer,
Planting seeds of good moments throughout the whole year.
In this garden of glee, hearts open wide,
With laughter as our compass, and love as our guide.

Breaths of Memories

In the attic of my mind, I find,
Old shoes that squeak, a tie that's blind.
Laughter hangs in the dusty air,
As ghosts of my past do a little dance and stare.

A hamster wheel spins with thought,
Remnants of pranks that I once sought.
Jelly beans hidden behind the books,
Each color a story, come take a look!

Doodles on napkins, a chocolate stain,
Mixing up joy with just a pinch of pain.
Each corner blushes with sweet delight,
As I chase the shadows through the night.

In this charming chaos, memories gleam,
Like a wobbly chair in a wild daydream.
With every giggle, I build my frame,
In the funniest hall of my heart's own game.

Heart's Compass

There's a map inside me, directions askew,
Where X marks the spot on a baby blue shoe.
With arrows of laughter pointing the way,
To a treasure chest full of silly ballet.

Ticklish whispers behind closed doors,
Bursts of giggles as boredom soars.
Navigating mischief like a pirate's delight,
With a compass that spins every day and night.

A landscape of blunders, oh what a view,
Where sock puppets argue about the hue.
Sailing through moments with whimsical aims,
Oars made of jelly and sails sewn with claims.

So follow the giggles; they lead to the fun,
In this compass of chaos, I've surely won.
With each twist and turn, joy gets its say,
Mapping my heart in the silliest way.

A Whispering Canvas

Colors of mischief drip from the walls,
Where splatters of laughter echo in halls.
Brushes made of giggles, strokes of great cheer,
A masterpiece painted with nothing but near.

Every stroke tells a tale so absurd,
Of misunderstood cats and an Aunt with a bird.
Balloon animals dancing around on their toes,
Under the guise of a painting nobody knows.

Canvas of memories, splashed bright and wide,
With splashes of humor that cannot hide.
In the gallery heart, I roam day and night,
Searching for chuckles that feel just right.

So let's roll the canvas and giggle some more,
Creating a world where the funny can soar.
With colors that whisper tales yet to be told,
In the laughter-laden art that never gets old.

Daze of Connection

In a world of wires, we tap and we type,
Sending silly memes that all feel ripe.
A dance of pixels, a virtual cheer,
Who knew connections could feel so near?

Silly selfies with goofy grins,
Tangled in filters that lead to wins.
A parade of friends on a glowing screen,
Where laughter's the language, and joy's ever keen.

With a poke and a prod, we make our mark,
In the digital playground, no need for a park.
Heartbeat emojis bouncing like balls,
Together we stand, even if through the walls.

So here's to the daze where we all intertwine,
In a tapestry of laughter, ever so fine.
Building connections with every laugh shared,
In this zany realm, we're truly prepared.

The Heart's Quiet Retreat

In a corner where giggles sprawl,
A couch that's both soft and tall.
With snacks piled high like a mountain's crest,
It's the best of the best, forget the rest!

Where socks go to hide, they party all night,
With a dusty old book that's lost its bite.
A rubber ducky named Quackle sits,
And judges my taste in comedy skits.

The cat and I share our biggest dreams,
To rule the world with ice cream streams.
While my stash of candy's under a bed,
It's the fortress that shields my sweet tooth's dread.

Oh, the laughter's too loud, the fun never ends,
As we plot with my plush little friends.
With silly jokes and pies in the sky,
In this sacred space, I'm free to fly!

Sanctuary of Unraveled Wishes

A fortress of pillows, a blanket fort strong,
Where I dance in my jammies to a silly song.
The walls are adorned (with sticky notes bright),
Each scribbled wish brings me pure delight.

There's a chair that squeaks like a stubborn old man,
And yet, it's my throne, oh yes, that's the plan!
A jar full of dreams sits on the shelf,
But heck, they're for friends, I can't eat them myself!

The lights twinkle like stars, though they came from a box,
And the clock tries to tick, but it just mocks.
I've got a remote to control my sweet fate,
But it only rewinds my last dinner plate.

With laughter and giggles beneath the moonlight,
I'm the queen of this realm, my heart's full of light!
Each wish becomes real, each thought a delight,
In this silly haven, I'm taking flight!

Lullabies in My Core

In the depths of my heart, there's a chorus so fine,
Of mischievous whispers and lovebirds divine.
They sing of adventures, of pies and of cakes,
With a wink and a laugh, for goodness' sakes!

A stuffed giraffe with a voice like a bell,
Tells stories of fanciful lands where I dwell.
With each note I hear, my spirit takes wing,
In this frolicking realm, my heart starts to sing.

There's a lollipop tree that grows in the night,
And candy-cane branches reach for new heights.
While jellybeans fall like the raindrops above,
Each one is a token of sweet little love!

Chasing dreams with a giggle, I swing through the air,
In a world of my making, I dance without care.
With lullabies echoing out from the inside,
I'm the joyful captain on this wild ride!

A Nest of Yearning Thoughts

A nest made of noodles, warm and quite cozy,
Where dreams dance around all wobbly and dozy.
In a pot of ideas, they bubble and sway,
Each one a noodle, in its own funny way.

There's a bird with a beak that only speaks puns,
While I laugh too loud, thinking this is all fun.
He tells me my socks are truly a sight,
With polka dots proudly worn day and night!

The walls are adorned with the quirkiest art,
Composed by my cat, who's a true work of heart.
Fuzzy thoughts drift like balloons in the breeze,
I chase them around, working hard to appease!

In this nest of musings, my spirit is free,
A delightful circus, come join the spree!
With laughter and quirks, my heart truly glows,
In this whimsical hideout, anything goes!

www.ingramcontent.com/pod-product-compliance
Lightning Source LLC
Chambersburg PA
CBHW060135230426
43661CB00003B/436